P9-DXO-536

SECOND HELPINGS
OF
CREAM AND BREAD

SECOND HELPINGS
OF
CREAM AND BREAD

BY
JANET LETNES MARTIN and ALLEN TODNEM

Illustrated By
ALLEN TODNEM

REDBIRD PRODUCTIONS
Box 363
Hastings, MN 55033

Copyright ©1986 Janet Letnes Martin and Allen Todnem.
Library of Congress Catalog Card Number 86-60390
International Standard Book Number 0-9613437-1-0

Printed in the United States of America.
All rights reserved. No part of this book may be used or reproduced
in any manner without written permission from the publisher.

REDBIRD PRODUCTIONS
Box 363
Hastings, MN 55033

This book is dedicated to our mothers who, without fail, served us *Second Helpings of Cream and Bread.*

ACKNOWLEDGEMENTS

— To Eunice Wold Pearson, our editor.

— To Andrea Syltie and Farid Saed for their photography work.

— To the Minnesota Historical Society for the use of their photos.

— To Hal Rindal for giving us the title to the book.

— To our families and friends for their support, ideas and encouragement.

— To our mothers for serving SECOND HELPINGS OF CREAM AND BREAD.

PREFACE

To say the least, we were overwhelmed by the success of our first book, *Cream and Bread*. Because a large percentage of our readers wrote and said *Cream and Bread* was good but didn't fill them up, we in good conscience could only do what a good Scandinavian cook would do—give them *Second Helpings of Cream and Bread*.

Second Helpings of Cream and Bread is divided into two parts. Part I—Food for the Mind—will surely give you a mind's eye view of the thought processes of Scandinavians through more diaries, a mortician's report, poems, and slightly exaggerated humorous observations. Part II—Food for the Body—is literally a gastronomical feast of the whole Scandinavian cooking scene and what went with it.

But, if after reading *Second Helpings of Cream and Bread* you're still not satisfied, our next book, *Come, Now, Let's Sit Down Again* will really hit the spot. And if you are one of those Scandinavians who just can't seem to get enough of a good thing, we've got another book on the back burner, too! *Leftovers* will be saved—just for you.

Now, vaer sa god, fill your plates and happy (eating) reading!

CONTENTS

Part II—FOOD FOR THE BODY

Part One

INTRODUCTION

In our first book, *Cream and Bread*, we printed a chapter entitled "The Diary of Lars Olson." Lars, on the suggestion given him by his pastor one Sunday morning, had written down his thoughts in a diary. After he was dead and long gone, serious students of Norwegian history found his private diary during a dig around his barnyard. And the mystery of what makes a Norwegian grin and bear it finally started to unravel. Lars forgot to close the gate, and the cows were let out of the barn.

But more was in store, and boy were they excited when the diary of Mabel Olson, Lar's wife, turned up intact, but a little dirty, underneath the chicken coup. It was comparable to finding fourteen double yolkers in one day. They were beginning to crack the egg!

But, that wasn't all! When the children of Ole and Myrtle Rasmussen, Bev, Carol and Ole, Jr. along with his wife Maria, auctioned off some of Ole and Myrtle's possessions after they were dead, serious students of Norwegian history found their diaries[1] and a couple of letters written by Myrtle Rasmussen. It was a bonanza of a bumper crop for them.

However, the biggest jackpot in all of recorded history was when an article published by the *Neo-Norwegian Liberal Journal of Medicine* came out of the blue. This article stated that Mabel Olson had agreed to have an autopsy performed on the brain of her husband Lars. According to one neigh-

---

[1]It must have been one crackerjack of a sermon that got them all to write.

bor who didn't want to be identified, Mabel was talked into the autopsy because she wasn't quite sure what it was all about and was too embarrassed to ask questions about such a personal matter as this. The unidentified neighbor thought that Mabel believed that an autopsy had something to do with the lunch at the funeral. So she told the mortician, "Vaer sa god."[2] She was confused that day and had a lot of things on her mind. Besides, she had never written a check so one couldn't expect her to be on top of everything.

It was a good thing that she didn't know that the results of this autopsy—which were underhandedly sold to the University of Norway mental health people for money—would be published. She would have been mortified. And poor Lars! He would have turned over several times in his grave if he had known. He wasn't ever comfortable with open caskets where people stared for hours on end at their leisure.

We came to the conclusion that it would be in the best interest of all to reprint this autopsy report along with the other diaries and letters that were found. Would any of you find Noah's ark and not tell anyone? Besides, we are not telling you anything you couldn't find out for yourself from the serious students of Norwegian history.

[2]"Vaer sa god" means "Help yourself."

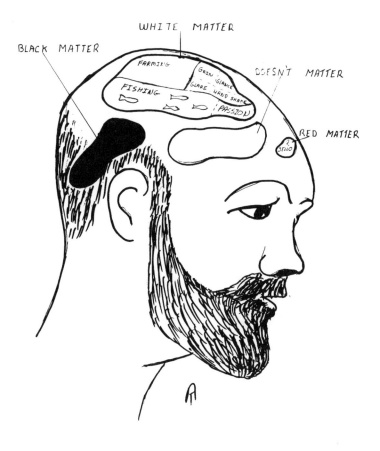

CHAPTER ONE

THE PSYCHOLOGY OF A SCANDINAVIAN: FACTS, MYTHS AND WONDERS

The brain of Lars Olson
was hard to explore,
A few major sections
was all it did store.

THE PSYCHOLOGY OF A SCANDINAVIAN: FACTS, MYTHS, AND WONDERS

The following is the complete autopsy report put together by a committee of morticians who examined the brain of Lars Olson:

"The brain of the deceased, Lars Olson, was filled with facts, myths, and wonders. After reviewing the following report, the reader might wonder if this is fact or myth. But we are giving you the honest to goodness truth. This brain was the most rigid, stiff, and stubborn thing we had ever seen in our lives. It was extremely difficult to probe and didn't give, budge, or bend an inch.

"This brain contained three major matters: (1) White Matter (2) Red Matter and (3) Black Matter. Unlike other brains, we couldn't find any gray matter. As a matter of fact, the bulk of the brain was pretty much all black and white.

"The *White Matter* was the biggest township of all. It covered four sections—farming, fishing, passion, and communication. We began our work by plowing through the deep furrows of the farming section. Cultivation was difficult because of all the tree stumps and rocks that had surfaced. The fishing and passion sections were virtually one and the same. Because there was a big lake of water between them, we couldn't figure out where one started and one left off. This was a hard job to tackle because there were so many minnows floating around that we had to fish awhile before anything bit. But after a few nibbles we started to troll and came up with a Johnson rod and reel, several barometers, a couple of pick-ups, and a few barrels of lutefisk. In this section the day May 17th jumped out at us too. There was some disagreement among the committee as to whether it stood for the Syttende Mai celebrations that the deceased liked to attend or for the opening day of fishing season. The communication center was divided into four equal quarters—the grin, the glare, the glance, and the handshake. Since this section was basically nonverbal and a big blizzard was coming up in this township, we decided to move on to the *Red Matter*. Besides, no one had anything more to say.

"It took awhile for the red lights to come on concerning this township. However, we are uncertain if the red came from (1) all the jell-o the man ate at doings (2) pent up anger against the new red hymnals that were introduced in the late '50's (3) a Communist scare—i.e. better dead than red (4) a time in his life when he sowed some wild oats and painted the town red. However, we do know that likely one of those, if not all, left their red marks.

"The *Black Matter* was the township of personal problems. Since this area had only one section, we thought exploration would be easy. But when we found it buried so deeply, it became another matter. Everything was all blackened out except for the words that surfaced, 'Keep it to yourself for it isn't that bad. No one should know if you're happy or sad.' And if Lars Olson didn't want to talk about it, who were we to dig it out?" Besides, it really doesn't matter now anyway.

CHAPTER TWO

THE DIARY OF MABEL OLSON

*What's in your thoughts, your mind and heart
or deep in memory,
Is hard to hang out with the wash
for all the world to see.*

THE DIARY OF MABEL OLSON

January 9   The pastor in church today said that he thought it would help people understand themselves better if they wrote down their feelings and thoughts. I suppose I can try it for awhile. I am sure it won't do any good, but it can't . do any harm either. Besides I have nothing to do when Lars is taking his Sunday snooze anyway. Everything seems so quiet and cold now that the Christmas hustle and bustle is over. And I still feel guilty about doing any needlework on Sunday.

January 16   It was another cold and snowy week. Ole and Myrtle came over to visit on Tuesday. They didn't have much to say. Myrtle said she had been busy embroidering all week. I wonder what she is making. She never said. I served them bars with their coffee. I put a Nestle color rinse in my hair on Thursday. I was sure glad no one seemed like they noticed it in church today.

January 23   Ole and Myrtle's son married a Catholic who is a foreigner. My heart goes out to Myrtle. I heard Selma talking about it on the party line. Myrtle must have known when she was here last week. It's sure funny she didn't say anything. I suppose she thought it was none of my business. But she should have known that the news would get around sooner or later. The Pastor had a good sermon. I had a suspicion he was talking right at Myrtle's son Ole, Jr. when he gave the lesson on the prodigal son. Poor Myrtle. She's had a tough week.

January 30   I told Lars that I had never seen it as cold as

11

it was this week. He didn't answer me. I wonder if he agreed.

February 6 Thank goodness it warmed up a little this week. Even so, we sure can be thankful for heat and lights in this kind of weather. I cleaned all day Tuesday and had a group of neighbors in to organize a shower for Ole, Jr.'s wife, Maria. Even if she is Catholic, his people have been long standing members in the church. We planned the lunch and the games. I decided to get busy and embroider some dish-towels with the days of the week on. They say she doesn't know English so this might help her too.

February 13 I told Lars there was no way I was going to go to church in weather like this. So we didn't go.

February 20 I went to town with Lars on Friday. On Tuesday I set a red jell-o for Valentine's Day. Lars must have forgot. Oh well, he's so good in many other ways that I can't complain about something as foolish as that.

February 27 I've got a busy week coming up. I have to serve Ladies Aid on Thursday. I found out at the last minute. Ida is sick so I am taking her place. She's been sick for two weeks. You'd think she could have asked me last week so I wouldn't be so rushed. Oh well, it will all work out. They'll just have to eat what I get made and be satisfied.

March 5 Lars is getting spring fever. He says he should be able to get in the fields early. I sure hope so. There isn't much for him to do around here. It makes me a little nervous to always have him under foot. I had my missionary group in to plan a silver wedding anniversary doings for

Per and Thelma. It took a long time before we finally got settled who was going to bring what. I volunteered to bring an extra sheet cake in case they ran out of the anniversary cake. There get to be a lot of hungry men to feed.

March 12 There sure was a strange looking family in church today. And they didn't look Lutheran. I wonder if they were in the wrong church. I'm always too suspicious I suppose.

March 19 Lars was really upset when the lady from the census bureau was here. I didn't think she was asking anything too personal, but Lars sure did. I told him she was just doing her job. He said most of it was none of her business.

March 26 We had such a good time at the silver wedding anniversary for Per and Thelma. And to think Thelma could still get into her wedding dress. Per looked a little down. I wonder if he wasn't feeling well. The food was good and there was plenty of cake left to freeze for lunches this spring. It was so much fun to get out and see everyone after the long winter. A cousin gave a cute reading on "How to Preserve a Husband."

April 2 Easter came and went. We had Lars' brother and wife from town over for dinner. She brought a nice jell-o with for Sunday supper. They certainly get around for being retired. He's so good to take her up North to go fishing every summer.

April 9 It sure is getting busy around here with making

all these lunches and stuff. I'm glad Lars finally got out in the fields. I'm going to have to quit this writing for a while. Getting that garden in gets to be a bigger project every year.

November 1 Lars said we weren't going to go vote this year. There is nobody decent running anyway. Like he said, there is a small choice in rotten apples. It really doesn't matter to me anyway. I haven't paid much attention to what's going on. They all sound the same to me. Besides, I have plenty of handiwork to get ready for the Fall Festival.

November 7 Well, all the canning is finally done. We should have enough to last us the winter and a little bit longer if need be. The Jensen's are moving their house to town. It is so nice when both live long enough to get a rest. I imagine they will still come and visit us sometimes.

November 14 I served a funeral this week for John Johnson's wife's aunt. She really lived to be a ripe old age. Clean living they say, even if she never did join the church. The Severson clan was all there. I can't figure out for the life of me how they knew her. Maybe they had errands to do in town and just decided to come over and visit some of the people they figured would be there.

November 21 Well, I'm glad that the Fall Harvest Festival is over for another year. It seems like the old ones are the ones that always get stuck with the work. Those young women sure try to duck out as much as they can.

November 28 Today we got the once over again about money. It seems like the only thing solvent in the church is the Ladies Aid. Maybe if the women could control the purse strings, things wouldn't look so bleak.

December 5 Well, they had the doings in church to raise money for the new hymnals. What a shame with all the starving people in the world. The money could be put to better use, that's for sure. I don't know why the pastor agreed to have some slick, fast talking big shots come down to try sell us on this. I started my Christmas baking. I told Lars I was cutting down this year. There is no sense to all those sweets.

December 12 I only have 8 more kinds of cookies to make and I should be done. I had to send Lars uptown for some more flour and sugar. They sure know what they want for groceries. I got a bar of Yardley Lavender for an exchange gift at sewing club. I think I got one last year too. Oh well, it will save for when company comes.

December 19 Martin Olson died yesterday. I imagine that will be a big funeral. Just think of how cold it will be. I wonder what they will do if that blizzard that is predicted comes the day of his funeral. People are so busy right during Christmas it's a shame he couldn't have lasted a little longer.

December 27 We sure had our share of visitors this Christmas. Everyone seemed to be out and about. The church annual report came today. The Rasmussen's sure didn't go out of their way when it came to giving this year. Maybe they were so upset about Ole, Jr. that they thought, what's the use.

(We are reprinting "The Diary of Lars Olson" found in *Cream and Bread* for those of you who haven't read it.)

THE DIARY OF LARS OLSON

Keep it to yourself,
It isn't that bad.
No one should know if
You're happy or sad.

9 January Boy, it's cold. The pastor said in his sermon that it would be good if people wrote down their thoughts. It would get them to think more. I wonder what he meant by that Since I can't think of anything more to write, I guess there's no sense writing any more today.

16 January   Not much has happened since last time I wrote. It's still cold and besides we had 8 more inches of snow this week. Some say it might be a late spring. Ole Rasmussen came over to visit on Tuesday. He didn't have much to say. Lars Pederson's cow froze to death on Thursday. I suppose he'll get a new one.

23 January   My how time flies. We had a good sermon today. There was a real bad storm yesterday. Ole Rasmussen had more bad luck. They say his son is going to marry a Catholic. I suppose she will turn if she isn't too stubborn. You can never tell. Mabel said that there was some in church that needed to hear what the Pastor said. I wonder who she was thinking about. She never said.

30 January   It was 30 below this week. My it was cold. It was 15 degrees colder than last week. Mabel said she has never seen it so cold, but I think it has been that cold before. I never said anything though.

6 February   Thank goodness it is not as cold this week as it was last week. Mabel had some ladies in to organize a doings for Ole Rasmussen's son. Even if he is going to marry a Catholic, some say they should give her a shower in the Lutheran Church since Ole and his wife are members in good standing and Ole's grandfather was a charter member of the church.

13 February   We didn't make it to church today because of the weather. I wonder if it will ever quit snowing.

20 February   I went to town on Friday. It finally quit snowing. Lars Pederson bought a new manure spreader. I wonder if he ever got a new cow? He didn't say. Lars and I ate dinner at Myrtle's Cafe. We couldn't even get a little roast beef dinner. All she had was fish and three kinds of pie. I suppose it was for the Catholic trade. She won't have any business left if she acts like that.

27 February   Mabel says I have to eat early dinner on Thursday. I suppose, I said. She has to serve Ladies Aid in the afternoon. I might as well clean up and go to town then. We've had enough snow for awhile.

5 March   The weather has been pretty good this week. I think we can get in the fields early this spring if it stays decent like this. Mabel had some ladies in to plan a doings for Per and his wife. I don't know why there is such fussing about lunch. If each one would make 3 or 4 dozen open faced sandwiches, bring a jar of pickles and a cake it would be all settled.

12 March   There was a new family in church today. They sure didn't look Norwegian. The Mrs. had real dark hair. Mabel was a little suspicious of them. Ole's wife said they work in town and don't own any property. I hope they are not hoodlums.

19 March   A lady was here for the U.S. census. All those questions. It was none of her business to talk about all that. Ole said he didn't answer her questions either. She even got stuck in my driveway. She should know better than to come out in weather like this.

26 March   We had the doings for Per and his wife. It was their 25th wedding anniversary. Per looked mighty uncomfortable with his suit and tie on. He couldn't even roll up his sleeves all afternoon. Good thing it wasn't so hot out. All that fussing for nothing.

2 April   Next week I will be in the fields so I will quit this writing for awhile. The weather has held up pretty good this week.

7 November   Well we got the grain up and it wasn't a real good year. The hired man took off right during harvest. It's hard to find good help nowadays. Some say Ole Jensen is selling out and moving his house to town. I wonder what he'll do in town anyway. I suppose the Mrs. wants to move to town.

14 November   I think winter will be early this year. It snowed 5 inches this week. John Johnson's father-in-law's sister died this week. Mabel served her funeral even though she never really did join the church. They say it was old age.

21 November   We had the Fall Harvest Festival at church. Mabel has been fussing and stewing all week. We had such a good dinner, I just about told her.

28 November   The Pastor spoke on giving money today.

I think he should wait on that sermon until after the church report is out. He doesn't have to worry about money with everyone bringing him chickens and eggs and everything.

5 December They had a doings in church this week. It was cold outside too. One of the big shots was down to speak. He had us grinning, nodding, and shaking hands right in church. Per Johnson's wife was even laughing out loud. I don't like loud women. He thinks we need a new hymnal. What in the world would we do with the old ones? They're perfectly good. I think he should keep his new fangled ideas to himself and keep his nose out of our business.

12 December Mabel says we got to get a tree. I wonder why she's always in such a rush. She's so busy baking and fussing I don't know why she's thinking of that too. Especially with the way the weather is.

19 December We got our tree yesterday. Martin Olson died yesterday. It was real cold too. Some said they thought he would last till Christmas, but he didn't. Mabel says Johnson's Hardware has new pressure cookers. If she has one of them, I wonder what she'd do with all her spare time.

27 December We had a real good lutefisk for Christmas. We've had a lot of company, but no new news. The church annual report is out. Mabel says the Rasmussen's could have been a little bit more generous since their son married a Catholic and the church gave her a shower and everything. I wonder how long winter will last anyway.

CHAPTER THREE

THE DIARY OF OLE RASMUSSEN

*It seems to me I work all day
from sunup to sundown,
But when it rains, I get a break,
and meet my friends in town.*

THE DIARY OF OLE RASMUSSEN

9 January   Well, here goes. The pastor said we should write down our thoughts. It's a good thing nobody knows I'm doing this. I feel so foolish. I can't understand for the life of me what good this will do, but I'll try and see how it goes. It sure is quiet around here now that the kids have left. I kind of enjoy the peace. That Christmas rush is too much of a good thing for everybody. If it doesn't warm up pretty soon, everything will come to a standstill.

16 January   I went to visit Lars Olson last Tuesday. He didn't have much to say except that Lars Pederson's cow froze to death. I wonder why he didn't keep it in the barn. With weather like this, anything would freeze.

23 January   Well, it's been a week of weeks that's for sure. Ole, Jr. came home from the Navy with more than his sailor suit. He brought home a new wife. Myrtle is just out of sorts this week. We were sure shocked. She doesn't know how she is going to get up enough nerve to tell the neighbors that Ole, Jr. married a Catholic as well as a foreigner. One's bad enough, but when you have both, then that's really something. I told her she would have to get used to it. She said she would never get used to it. And then to make matters worse, we had a real bad storm this last week.

30 January   Well, even though it was 30 below all week long I got a few things done. Myrtle told me that I had to tell Ole, Jr. that if his new wife didn't turn, his farming days were over and he might as well find a job in town. I think

I got through to him. When he told me times had changed, I told him that two and two make four today just as they did in my Lord's time. Lars was over this week so I had to tell him about Ole, Jr.'s new wife. He said Mabel had already told him the bad news. He just shook his head and said he couldn't figure out this younger generation either.

6 February I guess Myrtle is in a stew this week because they are going to give a bridal shower for Maria. She's all worried that Maria will act stupid. I sure hope the girl appreciates it, Myrtle said to me. After all the free lunches she's been getting lately, you'd hope so. Ole, Jr. seems to have settled down a bit. I think he's going to have his hands full down the road with that girl.

13 February We got stuck going to church. Ole, Jr. pulled us out and we went over to his trailer. We should have never started out in the first place. Maria invited us in for dinner. She said she was fixing pizza pie. It sure looked like lefse someone had puked on to me. Poor Ole, Jr. I don't know how he can stand to eat that spicy junk. I don't know why she just doesn't fix potatoes and meat like everyone else.

20 February I looked at the Farmers' Almanac today. Looks like we're going to have quite a few more inches this winter. Ole, Jr. and Maria came over last Monday. The girl makes me plenty nervous the way she has to hug everybody. I try to keep my distance from her as much as I can. Just because it was Valentine's Day doesn't mean a person has to get carried away. She sure isn't down to earth, that's for sure.

27 February I have to drive Myrtle into town for Ladies Aid on Thursday. I suppose Maria will go with. Myrtle is always on edge with that girl around. You never know what she is going to do. It's a good thing the girl doesn't speak English very well. Then we really would be in hot water.

5 March Well, March came in like a lamb, so I suppose it will go out like a lion. I finally made it to the elevator this week and picked up my new calendar. With the weather the way it has been, I just don't get around like I should. Myrtle went over to Mabel's to plan a doings for Per and his wife.

12 March Maybe the Farmers' Almanac is off a little bit this year. The weather is sure holding up. There was a new family in church today. Myrtle said they work in town and don't own any property. They looked like they could have been relatives of Maria. It's about time the government closes the gates and doesn't let any more of those kind into this country. We have enough problems with the people we got. And then Ole, Jr. brings one more in. What was he thinking of anyway?

19 March Well, the census lady was here this week. I can't figure out for the life of me why they send a woman out to do a man's job. I didn't answer half of her dumb questions. I think she was just trying to be snoopy. I told her she didn't have to bother and count Maria since she wasn't even a citizen yet then. Of course she got stuck in my driveway so I had to go pull her out. She should know better than to come in March the way the weather changes. Lars said she got stuck in his driveway too and had asked the same dumb questions.

26 March   Well, we were in church three times this week — once for Lent, once for church, and once for Per's wedding anniversary doings. Boy, he looked miserable. I think if the women had more to do in the winter they wouldn't be drumming up these dumb parties.

2 April   Well, the girls came home for Easter. Myrtle was just fussing and stewing over everything again. Maria brought over another spicy salad for Easter. I can't eat that stuff. I don't know when the girl will learn not to make things that go to waste. I don't care what she thinks. Anchovies are not the same as herring. Next week I should be in the fields if the weather goes right.

9 April   Well, I sure worked hard in the fields this week. It really felt good to get out of the house and have some peace and quiet. I'm going to quit this writing for awhile. I can't imagine what good it has done. Besides next week I'm going to have to get my shoe boxes out to do my tax work. I told Mabel to clear off the dining room table so I could start.

7 November   Well, the crop's up, and it could have been better. I started to bank the house this week. Ole, Jr. helped me hoist all those bales. Maria sat and watched. I don't know why she doesn't stay in the house where she belongs.

14 November   Went to Brotherhood this week. Mabel

served. I lost a rubber. On Thursday Mabel served a funeral. We didn't know the woman very well.

21 November We went to the Fall Harvest Festival this week. We had another good dinner.

28 November The Pastor spoke on giving money today. I told Myrtle he sure tries hard enough to get blood out of a turnip. We went down to Bev's this week for Thanksgiving. I sure don't like the big cities. There is nothing to do there and all those people. I can't understand why anyone would want to live there. They sure have their share of fender benders too. I'm sure glad it was only for one day.

5 December It looks like we're going to be hog tied into getting those new hymnals. There were even some big shots down to try to cram their ideas down our throats by acting like they knew so much. But Lars hit the nail on the head when he said they put their pants on the same way we do. I think we need a new furnace before anything.

12 December I've had such a bad cold this week that I don't have much to write about. You can sure tell it's getting to be winter. I feel it in my bones.

19 December Martin Olson died yesterday right in the middle of a cold spell. I just saw him a few days ago. I didn't think he had much time left but thought he would last until Christmas at least. Myrtle is busy buying Christmas gifts. I hope she doesn't buy me anything. There isn't a thing I need. I suppose Maria will try to bring in some of her traditions. We don't need anything new or different at Christmas. It's enough of a commotion the way it is.

27 December   Well, the lutefisk was pretty good. Everybody was home for Christmas. Maria was going around hugging everybody again. She makes such a big deal out of nothing. The church annual report came this week. There sure were a lot of surprises. Myrtle figured that most gave the same as last year. She sure has a memory to remember all of that.

CHAPTER FOUR

THE DIARY OF MYRTLE RASMUSSEN

*Life is hard and not so fun
when things don't go your way,
Thoughts should all be written down
is what the Prest did say.*

THE DIARY OF MYRTLE RASMUSSEN

January 9 When the Pastor said in his sermon that people should start to write down their thoughts, I'm sure he took everyone by surprise. I bet there isn't a man in the whole congregation who will bother with that nonsense! I'm going to try it for awhile and see how it goes. I have to write the news to the girls anyway so I might as well.

January 16 It was cold so I embroidered all week. It sure has been an awfully long day today. We went to visit the Olson's on Tuesday. Mabel served some good bars and some of her Christmas baking. I wonder why that woman makes all that stuff for just two people? She sure is getting gray. I suppose they're not so young any more either.

January 23 I've sure had the wind knocked out of my sails this week. Ole, Jr. shocked us all and brought home a wife from a town in Italy where he was stationed. I just couldn't get anything done this week. I wonder where we went wrong. He must have lost all his senses to think that he could do something as drastic as getting married without even telling us. You'd think he would have had the decency to at least write. He didn't even give us a chance to warn him. How could he expect anything but a cold shoulder? To go against everything he was ever taught in Confirmation and marry a Catholic is more than I can handle right now. I don't know how I am going to get up the nerve to tell the neighbors. I'll never be able to live this one down. I couldn't face anyone in church today—so I didn't go.

January 30 Ole and I had a talk with Ole, Jr. I told him he wasn't the same boy we raised. He said times had changed, but I'm glad his dad set him straight on that. I don't even feel comfortable going over to his trailer now that she's there. She can't speak English, she can't cook, and she knows nothing about farming. She must have wanted a free lunch ticket out of life, that's what I think. She'll just have to learn to work hard if she's going to adjust here. Lars was over and seemed to know all about it. I suppose Mabel was rubber-necking. It doesn't seem to bother Ole, Jr. to call the whole county and let them know. We did everything possible for the boy, and now he turns on us when we are getting older. I wrote and let the girls know the whole truth. I haven't heard from them yet, but I suppose they're in as much shock as we are.

February 6 Mabel called this week and said they are going to give Maria a shower in the church. I don't imagine too many will bother to show up. They asked what she needed. I said she needed everything for the kitchen. The girl will be starting from scratch. I cleaned out my basement and got a box of jars and lids put together for her. I suppose I'll have to teach her everything. I hope she keeps her mouth shut at the shower.

February 13 I told Ole we should never have started out to church in weather like this, but he didn't listen. He didn't have too much to say, though, when we got stuck. Ole, Jr. pulled us out and Maria invited us in for dinner. She was fixing pizza pie. Can you imagine having that foreign dish for Sunday dinner? Ole could hardly touch it. You can't blame him. It looked awful and tasted worse. It was spicy enough to burn anyone's tongue. Ole, Jr. looks like he has been losing weight. Who wouldn't with the stuff she serves? I hope he doesn't get sick.

February 20 I heard from both the girls this week. I don't know what's wrong with them either. Even though they were surprised to know that their brother was married, they didn't seem bothered a bit by it. I don't know what this world is coming to anyway. Maria and Ole, Jr. came over for Valentine's Day. You would have thought it was the fourth of July the way she carried on. She said she would have loved to have hired a crop duster to write, "I love you, Ole, Jr.," in the sky. I just glared at her and told her we don't do things like that around here. We would have been the laughing stock of the whole county. Ole, Jr. turned as red as the jell-o on the table. He must get awful tired and embarrassed with that woman.

February 27 Well, Maria just had to go with me to Aid on Thursday. We had a good lesson, but the girl made me so nervous I couldn't concentrate.

March 5 I went over to Mabel's to help plan the silver wedding anniversary doings for Per and Thelma. It took awhile, but we got all the food divided out. Mabel served leftover Christmas cookies with coffee. That woman has to learn not to bake so much. She probably didn't have much time to make anything else since she got called on to serve Aid at the last minute.

March 12   Well, we saw the new family in church today. I heard they live in town and don't own any property. I can't understand why they moved here in the first place. There is really nothing here for them to do. They just don't look like they belong. I started spring housecleaning this week. What a chore.

March 19   Ole was all upset about the census lady that was here. He sure lets little things bother him lately. Maria brought over some meatballs for us to try one night. Nobody liked them. I asked what she did to them, and she said she mixed a little oregano with them. I told her all we used was allspice. I think I got across to her that we like plain food here. I must admit she's starting to come around though.

March 26   I guess I'll take back my words from last week. Maria brought spaghetti to the silver wedding anniversary celebration for Per and Thelma. I was so embarrassed I didn't know what to do. Everyone else had tuna and cream of mushroom hotdishes, and she showed up with that awful red stuff. I don't know when the girl will ever learn. I worked on my napkin collection this week.

April 2   Well, the whole family was home for Easter. It was good to see the girls and the grandchildren again. My, the grandkids had grown. Everything went fine except we were blessed with another one of Maria's Italian salads. Oh well, I guess she meant well. The girls said they thought her salad was really good. I'm sure they were just trying to be nice and keep peace.

April 9 Ole finally got out in the fields this week. Even though it's early, it sure is good to have him out and about. Ole said Maria was outside barefoot one day. That girl is going to get sick if she doesn't watch out. We could still have snow.

April 16 It's time for me to put away this writing for a few months. I have to get the garden going and all the windows washed.

November 7 Well, the canning is all done. It took longer this year. I had to teach Maria how to put up things for the winter. I must admit she's been pretty good about working even though she likes to sleep till 8 in the morning. The day is half gone by then, I told her. The harvest is done, but the prices are down again.

November 14 I served a funeral this week—an old aunt of John Johnson's wife. Olga G. was supposed to help serve too. She never showed up or let anybody know why. I wonder what she would think if someone pulled that trick on her. That young Mrs. Ben Nelson showed up again with a cake we all knew she had made from a box. She is so extravagant. She's got all the time in the world. Some say she is just plain lazy.

November 21 We sure were busy at the Fall Harvest Festival. The Aid raised enough money to tide us over for another year. Maria bought a handiwork sampler that said "Bridal cooking is quickly learned; The coffee's done when the toast is burned." It was sure fitting, I'll say that much.

November 28 I got a headache listening to the pastor talk about money again. Every year he brings it up, and it's the same thing year after year. I think he should just stick to the Gospel.

December 5 If they think they are going to take all our Aid money to buy hymnals, they've got another thing coming. We need some new tablecloths long before we need any hymnals. If we would have known this was in the works, we would never have given all that money in memory of Ole's father for the old ones. I'm teaching Maria how to make lefse. She said she was going to make some Italian goodies this Christmas. I sure hope she doesn't box them up for the shut-ins. They just like the regular stuff. They're not used to anything different.

December 12 I've been baking and cleaning all week. It seems like I didn't get anything else done. We had our sewing club Christmas party. I got a new box of seamed nylons. At least it was something practical.

December 19 I started Christmas shopping. I bought Maria and Ole, Jr. a krumkake iron. Martin Olson had to up and die right during the busiest time of the year.

December 27 Well, Christmas is over for another year. I was worried I wasn't going to get everything done. The kids were all home so there sure was a lot of commotion around. Maria and Ole, Jr. came over before Christmas services. She was all decked out in a new red sheath. She had gotten a tube of fire-red Hazel Bishop lipstick and had smeared herself up good. I wanted to tell her to go wash her face. For crying out loud, we were going to Christmas services, not a celebration. The church annual report came today. Most didn't give any more than last year. That should tell them we don't want any new hymnals.

CHAPTER FIVE

LETTERS FROM HOME

*It's hard to think
Of things to say;
Dishes are done,
It snowed today.*

*Vern's brother died,
A cow did too,
Jon's cat came home,
Pa has the flue.
(So how are you?)*

LETTERS FROM HOME

Sunday afternoon

Dear Bev and family,

Just got the Sunday dinner dishes done and thought I'd get your letter written. We had leftovers. Church was half empty today. We have a little rain and some don't show up. I'm sending this with little John's birthday card. My, he's already 13. With the price of postage nowadays, one has to save where they can. And then they say it's going up.

Not much has happened since last week. Per Hanson died on Tuesday, services on Friday. My group served. It was a pretty good-sized funeral. Kinda surprising and so many flowers it was a shame. I saw a lot of his brothers and sisters who I hadn't seen for years. John hasn't changed, but his wife Agnes has sure put on the weight. She was poured into her suit. I used to get Christmas cards from them when you kids were young. And of course Maria is still up to her old tricks again. I just about died at the visitation service of Per Hanson. You should have seen her going up to the corpse and touching it. The girl has no sense. She hardly knew the man and probably only met him once or twice. But to top it all off she shows up at his funeral too. It would have been better if Ole, Jr. would have put his foot down and told her to stay home. She wasn't helping in the kitchen so there was no reason in the world that she bothered to come. But she's good at showing up in places where she's not welcome.

Ethel and Mabel dropped by on Tuesday afternoon. I served coffee and lemon bars. Wednesday I went to church and helped scrub down the kitchen. Pastor got called to the

41

hospital. John Johnson had a stroke. They said he wouldn't make it through the night, but as of today he is still living. On Thursday night I made a huge chicken hotdish to serve at the funeral. Selma and Verona each brought one too. We had enough left over so I didn't have to make supper when I got home.

Pa and I went shopping on Saturday. He read about the storm you had on Wednesday and was wondering if you were one of the 35,000 people in the metro area that was without power for awhile. We had lunch at the bakery and then came home. It's rained for four days straight. I wonder if it will ever quit. Your dad said he read about the stabbing down there. He says you should watch the kids real close. I suppose you didn't know who that little girl was. He says there are too many kooks running around in the big city. We don't have to worry much about that here. But some say it's getting worse. Someone tipped over Ethel's garbage cans—pranksters I'm sure. People were sure stuff would start happening like that when they opened the new factory. All sorts of riffraff and junk moving into town. We sure don't see them in church though.

We don't know yet if we will be down for Thanksgiving. Pa worries about the roads and doesn't like to leave the cows at that time of the year. You know how it is, and then with the factory that opened up. If we do come down, if the weather holds out, it will be for just the day and we'll leave the next morning. You know your dad likes to keep busy, and there isn't much for him to do in the city, and then with the traffic and all. He likes to get home early to read the mail. Don't plan any shopping trips either. You asked in your last letter what we wanted for Christmas.

There isn't a thing we need. Dad says don't buy us anything. Save your money for college for the kids.

I don't have any more news. I have to get a letter off to your sister and then to Hilma H. She wrote three weeks ago and I haven't gotten her answered back yet.

Love, Mom

Monday A.M. John Johnson died last night. Alice just called. I'll write about the funeral next week and send the clipping.

Sunday afternoon

Dear Carol Ann,

I just got a letter off to your sister, and now I'll do yours before your dad gets up from his nap and I have to get him his coffee. It has rained for four days straight. As they say, when it rains, it pours. It sure has been a lazy day. I wonder when it will ever let up. Are you studying hard? I hope so. It's a crime what one has to pay for education these days. Did you enjoy those Brown Betty bars I sent? I sure hope so with the price of postage. It cost more to mail them than what it did to bake them. What a fright. And then Ole, Jr. said Maria was sending a card to the Pope. I told him that was a complete waste. I got the recipe from Olga H. Her sister had sent it from California, and Olga is going to put it in the new church cookbook. And then they say that postage is going up. I wonder where it will all end.

Church was half empty today. I've saved all the newspapers for you from September. I'm sending them back with Vern Jensen's son who attends that vocational school down there. I'm also sending your boots and mittens and that scarf that Aunt Elsie gave you last Christmas. I hunted high and low for that scarf and finally found it in the south room. The way things are going we're sure to have winter before Thanksgiving. Even though we pray for the harvest, we continue to hoe. It will be a race to get the corn out. Maybe you could take the bus over to his dorm and pick those things up. He's driving all the way out here to the farm to get them and I don't want to bother him too much. Kind of a quiet kid. He seems nice. He was home for his uncle's funeral. And you can't guess who else was there? Maria. Hugging and touching people she barely knew. She bawled so much she embarrassed everyone including the pastor. Have you ever heard the beat of it? And Ole, Jr. just sits there and thinks she's cute. I wonder what he ever saw in her anyway. There was more there at the funeral than I thought would show up. We thought that we would run out of food, but we didn't. We even had enough left over for supper at home. Your dad didn't go. He doesn't like funerals, you know, so he only goes to the ones that he has to.

Do you remember that Severson girl who graduated a couple of years before you—the one whose parents lived out north of town about 3 miles? I heard at the funeral that she is pregnant by that no good lazy Peterson boy. He couldn't hold down a job if he wanted to, and his dad sits up at the liquor store every night. I couldn't remember her too well so I looked her picture up in the annual. You wouldn't believe what it says under her picture. "With blushing face and twinkling eyes, someday she will take the prize." Well, she sure did—getting that Peterson kid!

I feel sorry for her, but she made her own bed, and now she will have to make the best of it. Her sister was no different.

Well, no more news around here. I have to get a letter off to Verona. Study hard and prove yourself. You know your dad isn't convinced that it is necessary to send girls to college. He says money doesn't grow on trees. But I told him it isn't enough in this day and age to be good—you must be good for something.

Love, Mom

Monday a.m. I forgot to tell you that John Johnson had a stroke. I heard that he died last night. I'll write about it next week.

CHAPTER SIX

MIXED MARRIAGES: A CASE STUDY

Mixed marriages were very few,
it was not a good thing to do.
Now Ole had guts,
some thought he was nuts,
The verdict is now up to you.

MIXED MARRIAGE: A CASE STUDY

There was plenty of commotion when you mixed a Swede and a Norsk or a real Lutheran and a German Lutheran, but when Ole Rasmussen, Jr. on returning home from his stint in the Navy, drove into the farmyard with his new Italian bride, Maria Ave de la Camponelli, you would have thought that the Reds from Russia had come into the park and sabatoged the ice cream stand at the annual ELC Sunday School picnic.

Even though Ole knew, without a doubt, that she would be as welcome as the pope preaching in the pulpit out in the prairie at Prince of Peace Lutheran, he married her anyway. But upon introducing his parents to his new bride Maria, who was fidgeting with her rosary that hung around her neck, he caught on real fast that she wasn't the only one that was going to be bearing a cross.

Poor Ole, Jr. The only thing he had going for him was that Maria didn't understand English. Therefore, she could be spared listening to his father threatening him that if she didn't turn, Ole, Jr. was through with farming, and his mother making it clear as day that no future grandchildren of hers would be crossing themselves in public.

It was tough sledding for Ole, Jr. It was as tough as putting a loaded grain truck in fourth and trying to make it up the hill. It was useless to try to convince Ole, Sr. and Myrtle that not all Italian Catholics would go to hell for not knowing the words to "A Mighty Fortress"; ideas just don't die overnight out in the Lutheran belt. And once again the fire was fueled when Maria not only showed up in red pants at the annual John Deere pancake feed and machinery show, but laughed right out loud in front of men and everything just before the movie "What's New This Year With the Green and Yellow?" started.

In time though, Ole, Jr. and Maria weathered the storm.[1] But Myrtle and Ole, Sr. never did. Myrtle didn't have any time for a girl who used a potato peeler instead of a paring knife, openly kept red wine in the refrigerator, and brought olives instead of bread and butters to funerals.

Ole, Sr. couldn't understand where they had gone wrong. According to him, the kid had everything going for him. Just a few years back, Ole, Jr. had not only won grand champion on his steer in the county fair and had taken second at the winter shows, but he was also the one who had pitched the shut-out between the Luther Leagues of Prince of Peace and First in '52. And now, seven years later, his boy didn't even as much as raise an eyebrow when Maria set a ceramic grotto two feet from their trailer, right in the middle of a bed of petunias, visible from the road for all the township to see. The girl had no shame whatsoever.

But the real shame, according to Ole, Sr. was that his boy had no remorse for marrying this girl who came from a country that fought against us in the big one (WW II). And to top it all off, he was strutting around like a rooster pumped up with teramyacin acting as if he were Martin Luther himself saying, "Here I stand, I couldn't do it any different." But, he sure could have done it differently, ac-

[1]This is only partially true. When you mix an Italian and a Norwegian you have yourself a fire and ice combination. A cold, frigid, unmoveable iceberg up against a red, hot, volatile volcano, makes for a no win explosive situation. And, as they say, everything doesn't come up smelling like roses.

cording to Ole, Sr. If the boy would have had any sense at all, he would have married that Johnson girl next door who was the sole heiress to a section of land within driving distance of his.

CHAPTER 7

BEN BJORNSON'S QUOTABLE QUOTES

Ben solves all the problems in town,
his advice everyone took.
They agreed his counsel was almost as good
as proverbs from the Good Book.

Ben Bjornson's Quotable Quotes

Scandinavians didn't trust most people who gave advice. Especially people like Confucius. How could they? He not only wasn't born anywhere near Trondheim but had never sat sixteen trucks deep at the farmer's co-op elevator smack dab in the middle of harvest when the wheat and the weather wouldn't wait. Just how could he know anything about patience that would make any sense to the Scandinavians? They didn't trust people like Bartlett either. Any man who sat around with a pen in his hand (when there was work to do) lifting phrases from dead men like Shakespeare, who never did a day's work in his life to begin with, certainly wouldn't have anything meaningful to say to them.

But they did have one of their own philosophers, Ben Bjornson. Now he made some sense. He had never taken assistance or asked for help. Anyone who could keep his cool in the middle of August in the John Deere implement shop when he heard that his combine part wouldn't be in stock for two more weeks had to be pretty level headed. Ben was their kind of man, and they felt comfortable with his wisdom.

The following are some of Ben's quotable quotes.

On trials and tribulation: If it ain't one thing, it's another.
On technology: If the good Lord wanted you to fly, he'd of given you wings.
On energy conservation: Shut the door. Were you born in a barn?
On illness: You'll live; it will heal.
On working hard: Hard work never killed anyone.
On bad weather: She's a corker.

On smoking: If God had meant for man to smoke, he'd of created him with smokestacks.

On depression: Pull yourself up by your boot straps.

On saying your peace (piece) well:[1] It takes a brave man to stand up and say his wife is wrong.

On commitments: We'll have to wait till Sunday to see what the weather brings then.

On humility: What makes you think you're so great? . . .

On recreation: If God had wanted a person to enjoy himself, he wouldn't of given him all this hard work.

On getting the job done: Take the bull by the horns.

On compliments: Shucks, that was nothing.

On show and tell: The back of the church annual report and a loud woman are one and the same — they're there for all the world to see.

On staying out of hot water: He who falls in the manure better clean up before he tries to walk on the clean kitchen floor.

On common sense: The optimist exclaims, "The glass is half-full!" The pessimist says, "The glass is half-empty!" The Scandinavian says, "They both look the same to me. That's nothing to get excited about."

On a good farmer: He's a man who can squeeze a crop out of a field of rocks.

On extravagence: If you can't find it in town, you don't need it.

On a bumper crop: Since Ben had never had, nor heard of a Scandinavian farmer who had had a bumper crop, he didn't have anything to say about it.

[1]Either spelling of the word peace/piece is acceptable. It just depends upon the way you interpret the quotation.

CHAPTER EIGHT

MIND YOUR MANNERS AND P'S AND Q'S
BY EMILY PETERSON

Answers to life were all cut and dried,
for some it was plain as day.
Emily Peterson had a favorite line
"Mind your manners and pray."

MIND YOUR MANNERS
AND YOUR P'S & Q's

BY EMILY PETERSON

Scandinavians believed there was only one right way to live—their way. From their vantage point, problems were either black or white, and solutions were cut and dried.

Emily Peterson, the forerunner of Emily Post[1] and Ann Landers, told it like it was. Even though she didn't play with face cards, she called a spade a spade. Scandinavians from all over sought her no-nonsense, common sense advice. The following letters are little samplers of her wisdom.

Dear Emily,

Some days I feel a little depressed. I'm up to my eyeballs in work and can't seem to get it done. I got a good husband and eight kids. It gets worse as I get older. What in the world should I do? Depressed

Dear Depressed,

Snap out of it, for crying out loud. With eight kids and a good husband who works hard to bring home the bacon, count your blessings.

[1]Some say Emily Post was a third cousin to Emily Peterson and stole her common sense ideas and used them for herself. If she did, like Emily's daughter said, "She'll pay for it someday."
Postscript: Even though Emily Peterson is dead and gone, her grand-niece Anna Anderson has taken over the pen! If you would like to read her advice, you will find her column in the Redbird Tidings. See back of book for details on receiving this newsletter.

Dear Emily,

A friend of mine insists on playing with face cards at home and in public. What should I say to her? Concerned for her Soul

Dear Concerned for her Soul,

Take her aside and explain to her gently that the devil is lurking in those face cards. If that doesn't work, have your birthday club get together and buy her a deck of Pit for her birthday. She will get so involved with the Pit cards that the face cards will be out of sight, out of mind.

Dear Emily,

The neighbor boy, who is Catholic, was shining up to my daughter at the 4-H Christmas party. How should I handle this? Perplexed

Dear Perplexed,

This is a problem you can't handle with kid gloves. Let her know that under no circumstance would you find a lion and a lamb in the same pen.

Dear Emily,

What are the consequences of a mixed marriage between an ELC'er and a German Lutheran? Just Wondering

Dear Just Wondering,

To begin with, there are plenty of problems just mixing a German and a Norwegian. As far as consequences go – would you want to deprive your children of attending their senior high baccalaureate service? Just think about it!

Dear Emily,

A divorcee has asked to join our homemakers' club. Just what in the world should we tell her? Committed to the Home Front

Dear Committed to the Home Front,

As you know, one bad apple spoils the whole bunch. Explain to her that she would feel out of place at the mixed couples' doings that the homemakers put together at Christmas. Encourage her to do some volunteer work at the nursing home to occupy her time.

Dear Emily,

My fiance's father is so terrible to drink! I'm afraid my future husband might follow in his father's footsteps one day. What should I do? Worried.

Dear Worried,

Marry him and you're only looking for trouble. Birds of a feather flock together. Lay it on the line and let him know that you will never touch the lips of the one whose lips have touched hard liquor.

Dear Emily,

The neighbor girl is in a family way. Should the church give her a shower even though she still isn't married? Concerned Committee

Dear Concerned Committee,

I sure wouldn't hold the shower in a church. There's a limit to what can properly go on there. If she's taking county assistance, she gets enough without working. If not, a little acknowledgement for the sake of the poor baby who had no control over the situation in the first place, would be in order. She made her own bed, now she'll have to lie in it.

Dear Emily,

The neighbor man lost his arm in the corn picker last Sunday. How can I be of help? Thinking of Others

Dear Thinking of Others,

People who work on Sunday usually get what's due them. Since we have to be so careful not to judge, a couple of hotdishes would be in order.

Dear Emily,

I see my neighbor putting perfectly good watermelon rinds in her garbage. Even though she's young, you'd think her mother would have taught her about thrift. Should I say anything to her? Waste Not, Want Not

Dear Waste Not, Want Not,

You bet your boots you should say something. Tell her that eating the watermelon and throwing out the rinds is no different than throwing the baby out with the bath water. Remind her of all the starving kids in Madagascar. Her mother probably would be horrified if she knew of her daughter's waste.

FIRST LUTHERAN CHURCH   LUNCH STAND

CHAPTER 9

COLOR ME BEAUTIFUL, COLOR ME WHITE

White was the color of most of the food,
The dress, the house, snow and the hair.
Scandinavians thought this would be good,
to avoid attention out there.

COLOR ME BEAUTIFUL,
COLOR ME WHITE

Scandinavians have an affinity for the color white. Show me a Scandinavian woman who wears bright dresses and fiery red fingernail polish,[1] and I'll show you a Scandinavian woman who has some Italian in her blood.

There is something about bright colors that make Scandinavians nervous. Historians trace it back to the time (pre-Viking era) when this tribe of white-haired, white-skinned people living among the white-tailed deer and white cedar trees in the snow covered mountains of North Norway with their goats and glaciers never saw any other color. And to this day they never have felt comfortable with vivid hues.[2]

The Scandinavian preference for white can be seen in their choices of food. A recent survey pointed out that lutefisk, lefse, fish balls, potatoes, onions, cabbage, rutabagas, flatbrod, buttermilk, cream cakes, fattigmand, glorified rice, rommegrot and, of course, cream and bread are among their favorites. And, to top it off, they use only one spice—salt. Colorful foods assimilated into the Scandinavian diet are immediately altered and adapted to tone them down.[3] Peas,

[1]Scandinavian women bought red nail polish for one reason—and one reason only. They used it to mark the bottoms of their dishes and pans that they brought to funerals and other doings. It held up better than masking tape.
[2]When Ole Rasmussen looked into a kaleidoscope that his grandson had received for Christmas, he just about went crazy. It took him three days of walking in the snow to get over it.
[3]As time went on, Scandinavian immigrants attended social events such as pot lucks and church suppers. This is when they started to dabble in such Italian cuisine as elbow macaroni. Heavy use of cream of mushroom soup came into vogue at this time.

salmon, and chipped beef are creamed. Homemade vegetable soup laden with colorful carrots is topped with dumplings. Strawberries and raspberries have cream poured over them. Marshmallows are put over squash, and corn is not only creamed but covered with crackers. Sugar and cream are dumped into coffee, and chocolate cake is enveloped in boiled white frosting. Even red jello doesn't go unscathed! By floating a banana on top and then covering it with whipped cream, the bright color is concealed.

But the love affair the Scandinavians have with the color white isn't just limited to their foods. It is reflected in their dress, religion, folklore—in fact, encompasses their entire being.

Historically, the Scandinavian woman never went in for show. Put her in a beige dress,[4] paint her fingernails with clear polish, splash on a dab of Evening in Paris, and that's about as much flash as you could ever expect to see. She was perfectly at ease with a white dish towel tied under her chin or slung over her shoulder. She painstakingly ironed her husband's white dress shirt and waited with great anticipation for Memorial Day when she could once again bring out her white shoes. White robes, Confirmation dresses, wedding gowns, and Baptismal outfits were all part of the white scene. When she succumbed and bought her

[4]Beige isn't white, but it was the closest thing to colorless that they could find. When Ole Rasmussen's Italian daughter-in-law, Maria, (See Chapter 6 on mixed marriages) showed up at Lars Olson's funeral decked out in a fuchsia-colored dress topped off with an aurora borealis brooch and earring set and black seamed nylons, talk about the scene it created in the basement of First Lutheran. You should have seen those nervous flushed-faced shuffling Scandinavians.

kids white bucks, she smiled approvingly as she watched them carefully powder those new shoes. She had an inborn passion for clean white clothes,[5] white lace tablecloths, and Scandinavian wool.

Scandinavian men were no different. Forget about purple passion. Blizzards and white-outs were about the only thing that excited them, and it still holds true today! They not only remembered a big storm to the third and fourth generation, but were also able to give so many insignificant details that it almost scared a person.[6] This is probably the reason that there were so many Andersens, Olsons, and Jensens heading up to Alaska during the gold rush. Actually, it had nothing to do with the anticipation of finding gold at all! The thought of blizzards, glaciers, and all that snow was enough to pull them out of the hills, valleys, and prairies in record numbers.[7] Just as the Norwegian and

[5]Early Scandinavian immigrants made their own soap to wash their clothes. (Soap recipe to be printed in next book.) As time went on, and TV came into the homes, Scandinavian women lost their senses and got swept away with slick advertising that told them things such as "Duz does everything," and "Fab washes clean clear through and deodorizes too."

[6]Ask them about the storm of '40, and they will all start talking at once. We are sure that Shakespeare who said, "So foul and fair a day I have not seen," would retract his words if, he had had to live through the big one in '40.

[7]The only other recorded time in history that they immigrated en masse was when they came from the Old Country. Letters from relatives already here writing about harsh winters where the blizzards were so bad that you couldn't see the barn from the house, were just too much to keep them "down on the farm." And then when they found out that the king (President) lived in a white house, it was just too much of a good thing.

Swedish lemmings had an innate nature to rush to the sea,[8] so Scandinavian men had an innate nature to rush anywhere that is cold and white. They knew in their hearts and minds that the closest place to heaven they could find on earth was the White Pass in Skagway, Alaska. And with the gold rush, they had an excuse for going. It was a classic case of whitewash.

In addition, religion somehow got mixed up with the Scandinavian's zealous fervor to keep things pure and white. Little did the big shots in the church know that the uproar caused by the introduction of the NEW RED hymnals had nothing to do with the music or liturgy at all. Who could imagine that the Lutheran Church would ever have agreed to have red-colored hymnals gracing their pew racks?[9] Besides, most Scandinavians felt that purchasing new hymnals was a total waste of money. They agreed that it was the white man's burden to send missionaries to Madagascar, and the money could better be spent there.

Finally, the Scandinavian preference for white was verified through their tales and stories. Any Scandinavian can tell you that Snow White was a Norwegian raised among the miners on da Iron Range in Northern Minnesota.[10] And

[8]The Eskimos explain the sudden appearance of the migrating lemmings by saying that they spiral down from heaven during a snowstorm. They used the same explanation when speaking about the Scandinavians migrating to Alaska.

[9]Red was a color associated with the devil and hussies. Having a bunch of bleeding liberals and communists telling us that we had to start chanting like the Catholics was enough to raise the ire of the stone dead—including Martin Luther. The Scandinavians were convinced that these hymnals would be nothing more than a bunch of white elephants.

[10]There are so many miners up on da Iron Range named Dopey and Grumpy that we are sure this is the true setting of this fairy tale.

then there is Hans Christian Andersen, a famous Dane, putting the white frosting on the cake with his famous tale of the ugly duckling who turned into a beautiful white swan. But the real clincher came when the biggest dream of Per Hansa in Ole Rolvaag's book, *Giants in the Earth*, was to get his wife a white framed house with a white picket fence around it. Now you know, without a doubt, that this story isn't a bunch of white lies.

CHAPTER 10

LEAVING THE NEST

Oh, your pa and I were talking,
it's time to leave the nest;
We need the time that we have left
to sit and take a rest.

LEAVING THE NEST

Oh, your pa and I were talking,
it's time to leave the nest;
We need the time that we have left
to sit and take a rest.

We hate to push you up and out,
you're only forty-four;
It's time that you went out yourself
beyond the farmhouse door.

It doesn't mean you can't come home,
your room is always there;
We pray that you can find someone
with whom that room to share.

We've always liked that Johnson girl
who lives just down the road;
Oh she was active in 4-H,
she cooked, she cleaned, she sewed.

She always looks at you so sweet
in church on Sunday morn;
They say she works just like a horse
when pickin' her dad's corn.

Her mom was Swede, her dad was too,
her folks were all fine stock;
We wish you'd hurry to her door
and knock and knock and knock.

Well I just know her mom has made
a quilt for her trousseau;
Do hurry on, just go court her,
she has no other beau.

We'll let you use our car tonight
if you go call on her;
And dress up in your Sunday clothes,
it's her you want to lure.

And if perchance she's right for you,
just call us up and tell;
And we will go right over there
to plan for wedding bells.

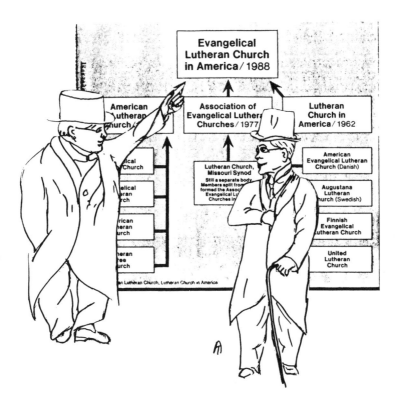

CHAPTER 11

THE MERGER

Oh I tell you Lars, you mark my word,
if this chart all comes true
There'll be so many changes made
we won't know what to do.

THE MERGER

When the Scandinavians immigrated from their Old Countries to the United States, they knew they were coming to a land where they would be free to work and free to worship. This would be their promised land, the land of the free and the brave, where they could be free enough to worship in any church and brave enough to start a new one if they didn't like what was going on in the other ones. And one only has to read a few pages of Lutheran church history to realize that there were an awful lot of brave Scandinavian souls!

Although the predominately Scandinavian Lutherans began to immigrate much later than Lutherans from other European countries, they were bound and determined to bring over their own brand of Lutheranism. And they felt no guilt pangs about not joining up with the already established Lutheran synods in this country. Even though the 1848 Evangelical Lutheran Synod of Indiana called itself the Olive Branch, names meant nothing, and by 1875 the Norwegians alone had managed to start five separate Norwegian church organizations in America. Some say that if Martin Luther had lived to witness this, he would never have turned!

Generally the Scandinavians, individually and corporately, had no qualms about turning from one synod and joining another, or freeing themselves from one in order to start a brand new one. After all, starting new synods was not a difficult task. If a couple of Hauges who moved into a community could start some murmurings, convict a few fence sitters to their way of thinking, grab a couple of Methodist-turned-Lutheran converts, they would have themselves not just a new church, but a new synod. And time and time again for various and sundry reasons, new synods sprouted up.

One of the biggest splits in the Lutheran church came when the issue of Predestination, or Election of Grace as it was known, came up for discussion. Things got heated and way out of control. There was even a rumor circulating that the Election of Grace had something to do with a forward lady who was trying to get her name on the ballot of the church council. Whatever the fuss was all about only the good Lord will ever know, but for Lutherans the Election of Grace issue became the *coup de grace*. New Lutheran churches and synods popped up like mushrooms, and the only thing they seemed to have in common was that they worshiped the same God.

It wasn't at all unusual to come into a small town and hear the bells of five Lutheran churches within a four block radius peeling "Faith of Our Fathers" at the same time. Even though the churches were dead ringers to one another in physical structure, inside they were singing a different tune.

But the civil war among Lutherans couldn't last forever. Healing was just around the corner.

In its infantile stages, the beginnings of the merger were subtle. The seeds were sown when the Scandinavian housewives, whether members of the Lutheran Free or Free Lutheran, bought herring in bulk from the same grocer. Swedish meatballs[1] were added to the menus of the annu-

[1]Some say that the introduction of Swedish meatballs to the menu of the annual Norwegian church lutefisk feed had nothing to do with the beginning of the merger at all. Disguised as a good will gesture in

al lutefisk feeds in Norwegian church basements. Norwegian Lutheran cookbooks printed recipes for Swedish rye bread. And the same beet pickle recipes showed up in both the Norwegian Evangelical and Augustana Free Lutheran church cookbooks.

The ever changing social scene indirectly fueled the fires of the merger. Both Danish and Swedish farmers bought fertilizer from the same Norwegian Free Lutheran elevator man. Norwegian insurance companies loosened their rules and allowed non-Norwegian spouses to buy term for a price. Lutheran town kids from various synods joined the same country 4-H clubs.[2] And the public school with all its secular activities became a breeding ground for the melting pot.

But nothing really took root until the advent of the hotdish. That was the impetus that set the wheels in motion for what was to become merger mania. Women discovered that by combining some new, varied, and peculiar ingredients, they could come up with some mighty palatable dishes. And, they thought, if such combinations produced those results in the kitchen, why not try a little potluck in the church? So they did, and they found out first hand that nothing happened when Luther Leaguers and Walther Leaguers got together to view Martin Luther films and eat Italian pizza pie.

---

the spirit of ecumenicalism, it was nothing but a way to get more paying people down to the church basement to fill the coffers. Even though the motives were questionable, the intentions were honorable since a certain percentage of the sales usually went for evangelism.

[2]Town kids, no matter what synod, never belonged to 4-H. They were usually Scouts. Country kids never did get used to town kids carrying their peach crates full of produce at the county fair.

Once the wheels started to churn, it was all uphill. People, sick and tired of separating, pulled their cream separator machines up from the cellars, out onto the lawns, and planted flowers in them as living reminders that they never again would separate. A committee of Lutherans even got together and put out a common hymnal. Unfortunately, while some embraced the books wholeheartedly, others paid them only token lip service .

Finally, most agreed that after generations of uniting, separating, and freeing themselves from one another, they had had enough. Besides, they could ill afford the chance of more separations because they were running out of ways to combine Lutheran with America, United, Free, and Evangelical. As a matter of fact, all possible combinations of those words had been used before.

After much debate, however, Scandinavian Lutherans came full circle when they settled on the Evangelical Lutheran Church in America as the name for the final merger.[3] But one only has to read Lutheran history to realize that an old Norwegian itinerant lay preacher named Elling Eielsen had the same idea 140 years ago when he established the first Lutheran Scandinavian synod. Even though it was popularly known as the Eielsen Synod, he called it the Evangelical Lutheran Church in America.

[3]It is preposterous to call this the final merger with some still holding out, though they may yet jump on the bandwagon. But then again, maybe not.

CHAPTER 12

GAMES PEOPLE PLAYED

There were many games played in winter by day
for men at the general store.
The only game left for my grandma to play
was cooking and cleaning the floor.

GAMES PEOPLE PLAYED

Oh, when we were young it was all done in fun,
the games we used to play:
Annie-Annie-Over, Red Rover, Red Rover,
and Pom Pom Pull Away.

Cowboys and Indians were often shot dead
out in the hills and the valleys;
But many a mother would never allow
the guns to come past our alleys.

Marbles came out when the snow went away,
cat eyes and steelies were won.
You had to be careful when you got home
not to let on what you'd done.

When we got older our games were much bolder,
excitement ran high in the streets.
The hot Chevy cars without mufflers or bars
played Chicken out there with the creeps.

The closest we came to a video game
was watching the TV screen.
On Sundays we'd rest to turn out like the best,
and lay in the grass and dream.

Face cards were thought to be sold, but not bought,
for gambling would be the result.
But, if you were sly, you could often get by
and just say it wasn't your fault.

The older folks, too, had the games they did play,
croquet and the horseshoes were fun.
Time spent on a tractor could well be the factor
for board games when day was done.

There were many games played in winter by day
for men at the general store.
The only game left for my grandma to play
was cooking and cleaning the floor.

The games may have changed, but the purpose remains,
to teach all how to be fair.
To have kids go straight even if there were eight,
showed all concerned that they cared.

Part Two

CHAPTER 13

A SHORT PROFILE OF
A SCANDINAVIAN COOK

Vaer sa god—the call was heard,
all up and down the streets.
Come now, let's sit down again,[1]
We haven't had our treats.

We're so full—the cry was heard,
we yust don't need no more.
Just a little something now,
you won't get lunch till 4:00.

[1]*Come Now, Let's Sit Down Again* is the title of our next book.

A PROFILE OF A
SCANDINAVIAN SHORT-ORDER COOK

A PROFILE OF A
SHORT SCANDINAVIAN COOK

A SHORT PROFILE OF A
SCANDINAVIAN COOK

Lars Webster defines a Scandinavian cook as (1) a woman who is as indispensable as a smooth running Massey Ferguson that doesn't break down during harvest, and (2) a saint who is required to do the impossible. Oscar Severtson's *Dictionary of English Synonyms* says of a Scandinavian cook—see martyr. But Ole says a Scandinavian cook is a strong neighbor girl you marry in order to help you out a little bit.[1] In retrospect, most historians agree with Webster.

None of these thrifty, industrious women, who didn't get time off when it rained, ever received any prestigious award for their accomplishments.[2] However, they knew

---

[1]When there weren't enough women to go around on the prairie, early "Ole immigrants" used to write and order over to the Old Country for cooks in the same manner they ordered their woolens from Sears and Roebuck.

[2]Even though we have never heard of a Scandinavian cook achieving any notoriety for her culinary skills, there was a rumor going around in Southern Wisconsin that an old woman from Prairie du Chien entered her famous Brown Betty bars in the Pillsbury Bake-Off, and Julia Child or another big-wig like her, up and stole the recipe and claimed it as her own.

they could run circles around the infamous French Chefs[3] who were fussed over continually.

Who but a Scandinavian woman could tell the grocer the difference between freestone and cling peaches,[4] hoist home a few lugs, can fifty quarts of sauce before the dew was off the grass, and get out to the fields to feed the men[5] at noon with a full four course meal topped off by a couple of warm graham cracker crust peach pies? Talk about beat the clock!

The Scandinavian cook, in all probability, could not tell the difference between sauteed potatoes or those that were *noisette* or *parmentier* shaped—but who cared? Who else, pray tell me, could tell you without batting an eyelash how many potatoes it takes to make potato salad for 100, or how much top milk and how many sugar lumps you need for a 200-person silver wedding anniversary celebration?[6] Who else knew, before she could write her name, what makes jelly gel, and that you can melt down salt pork, strain it through muslin cloth and have yourself a safe butter substitute for dark cakes? Who else would whip up six dozen funeral-sized

[3]Infamous French chefs are those who ooh and aah and stew over a single flute of Peach Cardinal. A Scandinavian cook would never fix Peach Cardinal in the first place. It sounds too much like what the Pope and his men might eat.

[4]As long as we're on peaches, we might as well bring in the topic of thrift. The Scandinavian cook not only saved and used the wrappers for a special treat in the outhouse, but she also often used the peach crates to make a vanity for her daughter who was at least of 4-H age.

[5]Bringing dinner to the men in the fields—food to go—was a fore-runner of Meals on Wheels.

[6]2½ pecks of potatoes, 6 quarts of top milk, and 2 pounds of loaf sugar

buns[7] in a day's notice to bring to church and not think it an infringement on her time? And who else would see that everyone else would have at least second helpings before she sat down to eat herself?[8] You could look high and low for a martyr of this magnitude. But the greatest virtue of a Scandinavian cook was her humility. Who else would respond to a compliment given her on a seven course dinner she served for fifty by saying, "Oh, that's nothing at all".

[7]Funeral sized buns were double the size of an ordinary bun. A Scandinavian cook was not intimidated by numbers, quantities, or requests. Ask anyone in all Christendom who has ever been in charge of the church lutefisk supper, or read for yourself a few pages up what fixing for crowds is all about.

[8]A Scandinavian woman wouldn't dream of sitting down to eat in her own home before all her guests had been served second helpings. A Scandinavian man, on the other hand, assumed it was his God-given right to eat lunch in his own home before any woman guest was served.

CHAPTER 14

FEEDING THE 5,000

Those tummies they just roll and groan
just like they always do,
Until the women bring the food
to set in front of you.

FEEDING THE 5,000

After saying, "I do", Anna Anderson had not only pledged herself to Ole, but to the pots, pans, and kettles. Feeding threshing crews and hired men, planning and preparing family reunion picnics,[1] church suppers, lutefisk feeds, and funeral lunches in addition to packing dinners in Karo syrup pails,[2] were just a few of her life-long commitments—not to mention frying potatoes in lard for the Mr. at 5:30 in the morning. In addition, gardening, butchering, canning, and freezing kept her turning in circles all day long.

The only thing she had going for her was that her people liked "ordinary food." The least of her worries was her spices. A little salt and pepper, a few pickling spices, an occasional onion and allspice for the Swedish meatballs was all she needed to make her food savory. She didn't have time to experiment with exotic spices such as oregano.[3] Besides, she had more important things to do—like finding enough zinc lids for the seventy-five quarts of string beans she was canning.

The typical Scandinavian diet revolved around the meat and potato scene. Food was plentiful, but plain. The typical well-stocked Scandinavian kitchen contained bins of the basic seven: flour, sugar, salt, lard, potatoes, cream, and

---

[1]An unwritten rule said that the family who lived on the home place was obligated to host a family reunion picnic one Sunday every summer.
[2]McDonalds got the idea of packing soggie sandwiches in a box from the Scandinavians who put those wax paper wrapped sandwiches in a Karo syrup pail. As they say, there is nothing new under the sun.
[3]Who needed oregano? You couldn't buy it in the store anyway.

eggs. From these foods just about anything could be made – and everything was. From lefse to cream sauce on lutefisk for the Swedes, from sugar cookies to potato pancakes,[4] you could always find a host of recipes that used those ingredients exclusively. But, as time and experimentation went on, an eighth ingredient was added to the basic seven – oatmeal. It was the most versatile food since the pontiac potato. Scandinavians not only used oatmeal to make breakfast mush which served as a side dish to meat, potatoes, and eggs, but they used it in breads, meatloaf, bars – and cookies that were dropped, forked, rolled, filled, and refrigerated. Oatmeal, a stretcher in a class all its own, was truly a miracle filler. And the Scandinavian cook needed all the miracles she could get.

For she knew that no roll of the dice[5] would ever change her lot in life, that of being the feeder of the multitudes, the nourisher of the 5,000. Even Norman Vincent Peale would have had a hard time drumming up enough possibility thinking to accomplish that.

[4]Some pronounced this "pan-a-cakes."
[5]This statement is a paradox. Scandinavians didn't roll dice unless they were playing monopoly.

CHAPTER 15

THE POTS, PANS, AND KETTLES

Oh our pots and pans and kettles
are filled up to the brim.
This food is not for those of you
who wish to keep so trim.

THE POTS, PANS, AND KETTLES

Oh our pots and pans and kettles
are filled up to the brim.
This food is not for those of you
who wish to keep so trim.

As once again we all sat down,
these goodies they were passed.
"Now help yourself," we heard again,
"And get some while they last."

Oh the coffee and fried chicken,
it all did taste so good.
We passed the food around and round,
and ate more than we should.

After all the food was eaten,
we took a little nap;
But then we woke right up again
to sounds of loud, loud taps.

When the women who were working
had cleaned the pots and pans,
They took and turned them upside down
and formed a kitchen band.

They played so loud we couldn't sleep
just lying on the ground;
They played so loud, the men were sure,
folks heard them way in town.

Oh the women all were happy,
oh they were having fun;
And they were pounding loud and clear,
'cuz all their work was done.

CHAPTER 16

FOOD FOR THOUGHT FROM COOKBOOKS PAST

To find a brand new recipe
sent the housewife on a search;
She always got the best results
in her cookbooks from the church.

FOOD FOR THOUGHT FROM COOKBOOKS PAST

The Scandinavian woman's ever-expanding social calendar of church and community potlucks put added demands and pressures upon her to produce hotdishes fit for a king. She needed more than just her pots, pans, kettles, and generations-old, cherished concoctions of the basic seven recipes if she were to drum up new tasty tuna delights.

But it was next to impossible to find a good collection of down-to-earth recipes. Betty Crocker was on the scene, but she wasn't much help. She and her side kicks were getting good money for cookbooks that told you how to boil eggs, cut up chickens, and a host of other common sense things that most Scandinavian eight-year-olds knew about. There were even ludicrous cookbooks flooding the market on such topics as candlelight dinners. Can you imagine someone trying to cash in on something the Scandinavians had eaten for years before the REA moved in? And surely those who promoted fifteen minute meals were nothing but a fraud. No one in the world, no matter how nimble, could get a six quart kettle of potatoes peeled in that amount of time—much less boiled!

Out of this frustration was born the church cookbook. Now those were real cookbooks! When you could find tips on canning crisp dills, hints on handling curdled milk in scalloped potatoes, methods to keep bacon grease from going rancid, along with eight different recipes for Trondheim Suppe, you had, as they say, "just what the cook ordered." And to put the frosting on the cake, half the cookbook proceeds went to missions.

Besides, these books didn't just contain fourteen run-of-the-mill, dull oatmeal cookie recipes. When you could find a recipe for Hollywood dressing and a section of VIP recipes, you had yourself a book with some razzle dazzle. Even though most of the recipes in the VIP section were a tad bit outlandish and no one took them too seriously, once and awhile you would come across one for a good chicken hotdish that the synod president's wife had fixed for the newly-elected district officers. But mostly this section just gave the ordinary person a glimpse of what the "powers that be" were eating.

Church cookbooks also had an international flavor. Little did the Scandinavian immigrant, who had brought over her tina full of salt pork and breads, dream that she would have her flatbrod recipe printed in a church cookbook 100 years later in the foreign dishes category! As they say, "You've come a long way, baby."[1] Since 98%[2] of this section's recipes contained Scandinavian goodies, it definitely came in handy at Christmas time. And the Scandinavian woman was really in her glory when she could find all rolled up in one book eighteen different lefse recipes with which to experiment.

The only dilemma most church cookbook committees faced was trying to decide the origin of a recipe turned in by thirteen different people. They resolved the $64,000 question by giving credit to everyone who submitted it—no ques-

---

[1]"You've come a long way baby," isn't being used in a derogatory sense. From Norway to the USA, was a long way.

[2]The other 2% consisted of mock chow mein hotdish recipes and others from the church supported missionary on the foreign mission field.

tions asked. After all, this was a church cookbook, and they had to naturally assume that everyone was honest.

The committee's way of insuring that everyone remained honest, hardworking, and above board was by printing some food for thought in and among the pages. They were little gems for daily living that ran the gamut from good clean living to preserving husbands and children. It was good psychology too, whether they knew it or not. A frazzled housewife preparing shipwreck hotdish for twenty-five in the middle of August found it so much easier when she could read the comforting words at the bottom of the page, "Life rough? Don't complain. Be like the robin singing in the rain." Even all the work and effort seemed worthwhile when she'd read, "There's something about a hotdish that makes a hit with men. They say, 'It sticks right to my ribs,' and fill their plates again."

However, a big percentage of the gems had to do with the housewife's duty in life—that of working hard to prove her worth. Those words that extolled Scandinavian virtues were no doubt what pulled her through many a tough time:

— Let us not pray for lighter burdens but for stronger backs.

— When you feel dog tired at night, it may be because you growled all day.

— Work is the yeast that raises the dough.

— If the going is real easy—beware! You may be headed downhill.

— If you are satisfied just to get by, step aside for the man who isn't.

— God gives every bird its food, but He doesn't throw it into the nest.

And lest she forget her priorities, one gem stood out among all the others:

— Housework is important, but not as important as religion.

AND MORE FOOD FOR THOUGHT

What makes jelly gel?
A recipe for love:

— 1 full moon

— 1 narrow beach

— 1 girl

— 1 boy

— 1 shady tree

— 1 cup of kisses

— 1/2 cup teasing

Method: Blend well in boy's arms. Beat it when mom and dad come home. Delicious served in the dark.

1 pkg. KOOL-AID, any flavor
1 pkg. Sure-Jell (or other fruit pectin)
3 cups Sugar (have measured and ready)
3 cups Water

1—Pour water into preserving kettle. Add KOOL-AID and pectin, stirring until thoroughly dissolved. Place kettle over fire, stirring constantly and bring to a rolling boil.

2—Add sugar quickly, stirring constantly. At first signs of active boil, remove from fire; skim quickly and pour into glasses before jelly sets. Makes 5 glasses.

KEEP *Kool-Aid* IN THE ICE BOX by the PITCHER FULL

This Pkg. Makes 2 Quarts

TO MAKE: Dissolve contents of this package in 2 quarts cold water. Sweeten to taste (about $1\frac{1}{2}$ cups sugar).

Store one or more flavors in coldest part of refrigerator —in milk bottles or new space-saving pitchers. Standing "ripens" flavor—more mellow, delicious. A healthful refresher, always chilled and ready. No ice cube fussing —no muss when children want thirst-quencher. Quick, handy, year 'round economy beverage.

For 1 Glass: Stir 1 level teaspoon KOOL-AID and 3 heaping teaspoons sugar in a glass of cold water. Serve iced.

107

CHAPTER 17

GRANDMA'S FAVORITE
SECOND HELPING RECIPES

Second helpings are a must
when feeding a big crew.
If the kettle gets too low,
. . . no leftovers[1] for you!

[1]*Leftovers*—title of our fourth book.

GRANDMA'S FAVORITE SECOND HELPING RECIPES

BAKED BEANS

For every cup of beans use 1 rounded tablespoon of brown sugar and 1 tablespoon molasses. Cover beans well with water and boil until hulls start to loosen. Add salt, sugar and molasses and 1 teaspoon dry mustard. Add bacon and a small onion and bake for at least 2 hours or more. 1 pound of beans = a roaster.

Selma Nestegard

Footnote: A must for family reunion picnics.

POTATO SALAD FOR 100

Boil up 32 pounds of potatoes. Chill. Add 4 bunches of celery, 4 dozen hard-boiled eggs, 8 green peppers, pickles, salad dressing and salt and pepper to taste. Recipe can be doubled for big crowds.

FRIED CHICKEN
FOR FAMILY REUNION PICNICS

Preparation: Go out to the chicken coop and find yourself about 14 old biddies who haven't been keeping up their end of the bargain as far as producing eggs goes. Bring them to the chopping block and axe off their heads. Let them flop around for awhile—half dead. Whip them into the kitchen, and immerse them in scalding water to loosen the feathers. Next, roll up a newspaper, set it on fire and singe the remaining feathers off. (This is done after you lift them out of the boiling water). Make sure you don't start anything else on fire!! Take all the innards out, and you're ready to start. (If you are planning to serve these chickens for a Sunday noon family reunion picnic, it's best you do the preparation on Saturday so you're not rushed.) Sunday morning—early a.m.—wash and cut up the 14 chickens. Wipe them dry, season with a little salt and pepper, dip them in beaten eggs and flour, and fry them in hot lard on top of the stove. After they are done frying, put them in a big roaster and let them finishing baking while you are at church. When you get home from church, you can take the drippings and make a little gravy.

Since this was the most popular recipe in our book, *Cream and Bread*, we thought we would reprint it for those of you who haven't read our last book. For family reunion picnics this recipe can be doubled.

JELLO FOR A CROWD

4 boxes jello
4 cups hot water.
4 cups cold water.

Dissolve jello in hot water. Be careful to get everything dissolved. Add cold water and refrigerate. When partially set, carefully slice in 1 good sized banana or 2 small. This will feed about 30 people and is good for funerals or other doings. (This recipe was used for the 75th anniversary of the Trinity Lutheran Church).

O Lutefisk . . . O Lutefisk . . . how fragrant your aroma
O Lutefisk . . . O Lutefisk . . . You put me in a coma.
You smell so strong . . . you look like glue
You taste yust like an overshoe
But Lutefisk. . . . come Saturday
I tink I'll eat you anyway.

"O Lutefisk", written by E. C. Stangland.
The poem taken from his book, O Lutefisk.

CHURCH BASEMENT LUTEFISK FEEDS

If there were ever justification for second helpings, it was at the annual church basement lutefisk feeds. After reading the following list of foods needed for one of these huge undertakings, you will know why the red-armed, tired women who prepared this feast were hustled out of the kitchen for a heartfelt round of applause.

Lutefisk dinner for 1200
600 pounds of lutefisk
400 pounds of meatballs
116 pounds of butter
600 pounds of potatoes
276 cans of corn
40 gallons of cold slaw
40 quarts of dill pickles
20 quarts of beet pickles
600 pieces of flatbrod
2,000 pieces of lefse
20 loaves of rye bread (for the Swedes)
60 dozen buns
3,500 cups of coffee
Between 5,000–6,000 Scandinavian cookies such as krumkake, spritz, etc.

Vaer sa god!!!

CHAPTER 18

VAER SA GOD—IT'S COFFEE TIME

Out, out the door went the ground coffee beans when new Chase & Sanborn came on the scene.

VAER SA GOD—IT'S COFFEE TIME

Scandinavians trace their vaer sa god coffee time roots back to Martin Luther. Anyone who could, after a hard day's work, stay up all night and pound ninety-five theses on a door had to get his strength from someplace. And they found out where it came from when he pulled out a thermos of egg coffee that Katherine had made and started attacking a group of Catholics who were on a diet of worms. He had literally hit the nail on the head, and from that time forth, no other liquid was treated with such reverence and importance.

Coffee was king. When the Scandinavian immigrants left the Old Country with their trunks full of survival necessities and their meager rations of flatbrod, salt, and side pork, there was always room for their coffee beans. You would have thought they were carrying a bag of gold nuggets. And when they settled in the hills and valleys of their new country, they made sure they followed the unwritten rule that whether one is sick or well, poor or rich, the pot should be on day or night in rain or shine.[1] They followed this principle to a tea even though tea never got the same respect as coffee. Nobody would think of playing a trick on you by saying, "Vaer sa god", and then hand you a cup of tea. Tea was for the sick, the wimps, and town women who thought they were from Hollywood.

Even though coffee was for the strong, the strong some-

---

[1]Shakespeare, himself even had trouble with this rule. When he said, "Double, double toil and trouble; Fire burn and cauldron bubble," one assumes he was talking about the trouble he was having one day making coffee.

times got served weak coffee—and boy did they complain! A good cup of strong coffee had enough hypnotic power in it to make a Scandinavian man temporarily forget about the price of wheat, potatoes, and corn—even if we're talking parity. But the women made it strong for another reason. It was the only thing that concealed the stains on the bottoms of the light colored melmac cups—stains as indelible as the black chapped line left on the calves of a woman's legs from tramping through four feet of snow in a new pair of kickerinos. Strong coffee also afforded the opportunity to get an additional kick from rolled sugar cookies and sugar lumps[2] that could be dunked. But, the biggest motive for making strong coffee was that it was the only justifiable reason found for dumping pints of cream and pounds of sugar in their cups.

In addition to strong and weak coffee, the Scandinavian ran up against some that was good and some that was bad. But no one lost out when it came to drinking funeral coffee, i.e. coffee boiled with raw eggs in white enameled pots. Just the smell of it drifting up to the sanctuary from the basement of First Lutheran was enough to make any good Lutheran pastor shorten up the service a bit so everyone could be ushered down the basement to get down to the business of what a funeral is all about anyway—eating and drinking coffee with the neighbors.

But whether coffee was strong or weak, good or bad, a certain mystique evolved concerning the art of pouring

[2]Sugar lumps, sometimes called lump suckers, were blocks of sugar about the size of dice that were often used as strainers. By putting a sugar lump between the upper and lower plates, a person could get a quick fix by sucking the coffee through it.

coffee at weddings or doings. When a person read in the local paper that "so and so poured," that was all that needed to be said. You knew that the woman who poured wasn't (1) pouring hard liquor and (2) she no doubt got a new dress and perm to sit at the end of the wedding buffet table to make sure that the men didn't try to run away with the saucer to the cup of coffee she had just poured. Pouring coffee at a doings wasn't a job you just gave to anyone. The coffee pourer at a wedding was just about as important as the mother of the groom. She usually got about the same size corsage which verified her status.

But the biggest status symbol on the prairie was the silver service set. Lucky was the woman who could nonchalantly say to the committee planning the lunch for the district convention to be held at their church, "I have a silver service you can use." Anyone who owned something that looked like it came from the White House was nothing but envied. A Scandinavian woman didn't care if she ever owned a fur coat or was taken on a cruise.[3] But a person could safely bet his last cup of coffee that a Scandinavian woman who owned a silver service[4] was as content as Thor, the Norwegian god of thunder who somehow got himself a 2 pound can of Mrs. Olson's Folgers regular grind. After brewing himself up a couple of gallons of coffee in his new Vaer Sa God rosmaled enameled coffee pot, he lay

[3]A cruise was the last thing a Scandinavian woman wanted. She still had fresh in her mind, the nightmares of floating around in the sea trying to get over here.
[4]Silver service sets were often bought with the dollar bills that were given couples at their silver wedding anniversary doings. That is, if things were going well on the farm. (For details of silver wedding anniversary doings, see *Cream and Bread*, Chapter 10—"Reflections on Silvers.")

back in the weeds as content as a cow grazing on a new patch of grass in the spring of the year, and started to drink. He drank so much he forgot to do his work, that of bringing the rain and thunder. And most Scandinavians will tell you that this was the reason for the dust bowls of the '30's that nearly wiped them out.

Even though coffee and the whole scene that went with it was of utmost importance to the Scandinavians, most of them will agree with good King Solomon that, "For everything there is a season, and a time for every matter under heaven."

CHAPTER 19

YOU'VE GOT TO KEEP YOUR STRENGTH UP

You've got to keep your strength up
by cleaning up your plates.
Eat up those second helpings,
before it's all too late.

YOU'VE GOT TO
KEEP YOUR STRENGTH UP

You've got to keep your strength up,
listen to what I say.
Listen very carefully
and life will go your way.

Oh, you're so very lucky
as lucky as can be.
You're nice and big and healthy
as all the world can see.

You've got to keep your strength up,
your pa is dead and gone.
It takes strong men to do the work
from sunup to sundown.

I've always worked so hard to feed
your pa and all you boys.
I gave you second helpings
so you would look so choice.

You've got to keep your strength up,
now listen up you boys.
Life is more than chevy cars
and all your boyhood toys.

Now all the girls are looking
at all my boys so strong.
I am so very proud of yous
and cook the whole day long.

You've got to keep your strength up
by cleaning up your plates.
Eat up those second helpings
before it's all too late.

AND A TESTIMONY FROM THE GRANDMOTHER OF THE BOYS!

Where do you think, that I would be
a little old lady of ninety three . . .

If I hadn't eaten the foods right for me,
I wouldn't be picking this apple tree (see photo)

If I hadn't worked myself to the bone,
I wouldn't be writing this cute little poem.

If I hadn't cleaned with homemade lye soap,
I would not have lived this long life of hope.

If I had not taken the time to share,
I'd be living alone with no one to care—

so

Keep up your strength, and you might be
. . . able to reach—ninety three!!!

CREDITS FOR ILLUSTRATIONS

Cover Picture—Minnesota Historical Society, Woman sampling food from pot on the stove.

Minnesota Historical Society, family reunion picnic, *page 93.*

Minnesota Historical Society, women cooking at stove, *page 109.*

Minnesota Historical Society, preparing lutefisk. Photo: *St. Paul Daily News*, *page 115.*

Minnesota Histocial Society, Stavanger Kaffestua, *page 117.*

Minnesota Historical Society, typical Finnish type farm woman, *page 126.*

ABOUT THE AUTHORS

Janet Martin, daughter of the late John and Helen Klemetson Letnes, grew up in the rural setting of Hillsboro, North Dakota. Both her maternal and paternal grandparents came from Norway and helped settle this area. She received her B.A. from Augsburg College, Minneapolis, Minnesota, and furthered her studies at the University of Minnesota. In 1983 Janet wrote a family history book entitled *Reiste Til Amerika*. In 1984 she co-authored a book with Allen Todnem entitled *Cream and Bread*. She and her husband, Neil Martin of Newfolden, Minnesota, reside in Hastings, Minnesota, with their three daughters, Jennifer, Sarah, and Katrina.

Allen Todnem, son of Krist and Cecelia Kallem Todnem, was born and raised in DeKalb, Illinois. His father immigrated to this country from Norway in 1926. Allen's maternal grandparents immigrated from Norway in the late 1800's and settled near Norway, Illinois. Allen attended Waldorf Jr. College, Forest City, Iowa, received his B.A. degree from Augsburg College, Minneapolis, Minnesota, and his M.A. from the University of Northern Iowa, Cedar Falls, Iowa. He is presently employed by the Hastings public school district as a senior high science teacher. In 1984 he co-authored a book with Janet Martin entitled *Cream and Bread*. Allen and his wife, Patty Holmen of Windom, Minnesota, reside in Hastings, Minnesota, with their three children, Eric, Danny, and Suzanne.

Reorder Form for *Cream and Bread*

Name _____

Address _____

_____ Zip _____

No. of Copies _____@ $7.95/copy   Subtotal _____

Postage & Handling $1.25   _____

MN Residents add 6% sales tax   TOTAL _____

Send cash, check or money order to Redbird Productions,
Box 363, Hastings, MN 55033.

For our free brochure and a copy of our new newsletter
"THE REDBIRD TIDINGS", send a self addressed stamped
envelope to the above address.

If you have not read our second book, *Second Helpings of
Cream and Bread*, you can order it from us at Redbird for
the price of $7.95 plus postage.

— ·— ·— ·— ·— ·— ·— ·— ·— ·— ·— ·— ·—

Reorder Form for *Cream and Bread*

Name _____

Address _____

_____ Zip _____

No. of Copies _____@ $7.95/copy   Subtotal _____

Postage & Handling $1.25   _____

MN Residents add 6% sales tax   TOTAL _____

Send cash, check or money order to Redbird Productions,
Box 363, Hastings, MN 55033.

For our free brochure and a copy of our new newsletter
"THE REDBIRD TIDINGS", send a self addressed stamped
envelope to the above address.

If you have not read our second book, *Second Helpings of
Cream and Bread*, you can order it from us at Redbird for
the price of $7.95 plus postage.

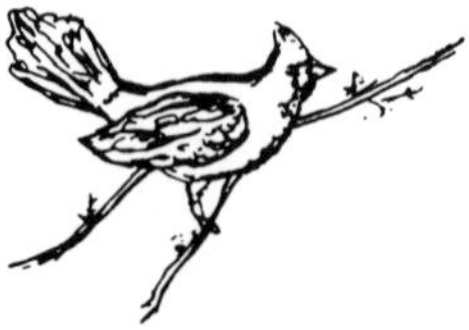

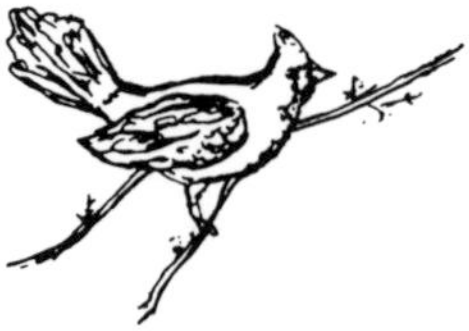